Cherry Blossoms

In Twilight

Memories of a Japanese Girl

Yaeko

八
恵
子

Yaeko Sugama Weldon

and Linda E. Austin

Moonbridge Publications
St. Louis, Missouri

Cherry Blossoms in Twilight

ISBN: 978-0-9772323-1-4

Library of Congress Control Number: 2006907969

First Edition, 2005
Second Edition, 2007

www.moonbridgebooks.com

For
Alaina, Kylie, Meghan and Cody

Every one of us is a book with a story worth telling.

—Kathleen G. Schultz

ACKNOWLEDGEMENTS

Thank you to my dear friend Frankie Haynes who thought my life was interesting and pushed me to start this book. She persuaded me to write about some of my memories to share with my family and friends. She read my broken-English writing and typed the stories the best she could.

Special thanks to my daughter Linda who took Frankie's work and made it into the story of my life. She reminded me of all the stories I told her when she was growing up, and asked me so many questions about so many things I thought no one would care to hear about.

I am grateful for the love and encouragement of my two daughters and all my wonderful friends who helped me in so many ways. I thank God for helping me through dark times by sending many "earth angels" to me. I have been blessed.

—Yaeko Sugama Weldon

Additional thanks to:

Kathleen Schultz
Stephanie Schlamb
Mr. & Mrs. Yoshiaki Shibusawa

Table of Contents

This book is full of the many memories of my life as I remember them now in my older years. Some are painful, but most are wonderful to me. They are treasures in my heart.

—Yaeko Sugama Weldon

Cherry Blossoms

In Twilight

Childhood

A long time ago, in 1925, I was born in the town of Tokorozawa in Saitama-Prefecture, Japan. It was a small town surrounded by farm fields. Nearby was the first airport ever built in Japan. From the back yard of my house, I could see in the far distance Mt. Fuji with snow on top. Only in the middle of the summer there was not snow. Also I could see the Chichibu mountain range spread as blue mist across the horizon. It was a beautiful view, and so peaceful. I could not imagine then how this peace would be broken.

My family lived on the main street of the town. There were small shops on both sides of the street. The shop owner families lived in the same building as their shops, either above or behind or next to their business. The shops and houses were right off of the street so there were no front yards, just the dirt road.

My father's shop was in part of the front area of our house. There was a sign up on our rooftop to advertise his business. Next door there was a small grocery that sold only very basic food that was stored in big wooden barrels. There was soy sauce, soybean paste, sugar, and sake wine. There was also candy and rice crackers kept in big glass jars on the counter. A bicycle shop was on the other side of our house. Across the street there was a tea shop that sold different kinds of dried green tea leaves in beautiful tin containers. Our street was busy with people walking or riding bicycles. Sometimes men would lead oxen pulling carts of grain or vegetables down the street.

We were poor and had a simple house, just a typical Japanese town house made of wood. It was one-story and had a tin roof so when rain came down we could hear loud raindrop noises. Two-inch thick straw "tatami" mats covered the wood floors. We had sliding "karakami" screens made of thick paper to divide the house into rooms. They were also used as closet doors. Some of the screens had beautiful paintings of scenery on them.

There were two rooms that we could make with the screens, and also a kitchen area. At night, we slept on the floor on soft futon mats. In the morning, we rolled up the heavy sleeping mats and put them in the closets. We had the closets and some wooden chests for storage.

When it was time to eat, the table was brought into the room. It had short legs that would fold up so it could store away easily. There were no chairs, just square cushions on the floor. We would sit on our knees on the cushions.

We had a typical Japanese-style bath room. It was a separate room with tile walls and a tile floor. The bathtub was about thirty inches deep and oval-shaped. It was made of cedar wood so it would not get warped and would last a long time. The sides of the tub were so high that we used a footstool to climb into it. We had to carry wooden buckets of water from the well in the backyard to fill the tub. At one end of the tub was a metal compartment to put hot coals in to warm the water. There was a metal pipe that went from the compartment up through the roof to let the smoke out.

We sat on a short stool to wash ourselves, outside of the bathtub. There was a faucet low on the wall and a drain in the tile floor. After washing, we sat in the tub to soak. We took turns washing and then using the same tub water to soak in. When I sat in the tub, the hot water covered my shoulders and felt so good. Once, in the winter while I was sitting in very hot bath water, my father scooped a shovelful of snow from our low rooftop and dumped it into the water and said, "That will make you cool!"

All the houses had small back yards that were mostly dirt, but with the humidity it was not too dusty. We had a large persimmon tree in the yard that made delicious sweet fruit in the fall. Japanese persimmons are much bigger than the American kind. My mother planted a few white rose bushes to climb on the short bamboo fence that went along the very back of our yard. We had a path made of flat round stones that went from the back door to a gate that my father had made. The gate had two wooden doors and a straw roof. It was a common style. We had an outhouse in the backyard, too. It was not fun to go to the outhouse in the middle of a cold winter night!

Behind our row of shops and houses was a dirt path, and across the path was a big field filled with mulberry bushes. A little stream went through the field. The water was very clear and cold. Farm workers picked the mulberry leaves to be shipped to the silkworm farms. Silkworms are moth caterpillars that only eat mulberry leaves.

Once my school class went to visit a silkworm farm and saw many shelves filled with caterpillars. There were so many eating the leaves that it sounded like soft rain falling. The caterpillars made cocoons that would be unraveled for the silk threads. Outside the tea shop, in season, farmers would bring big bamboo baskets full of silkworm cocoons and a man there would separate them by how good they looked. Buyers would come to bargain and take the cocoons to factories.

My father was a shoemaker. He had one man who worked for him. My father bargained with farmers for Paulownia trees. They are valuable in Japan. Wood from Paulownia trees is very light in weight, like air. My father made wooden "geta" shoes that are like sandals on short stilts, but the wood is also used to make Japanese-style chests-of-drawers, gift boxes, and other kinds of nice wooden objects.

My father had shoes on display for customers to walk in and buy, and also took orders from shoe stores. It was amazing to watch him making everything by hand, using many different kinds of tools. I used to help him polish the finished shoes with a small stiff brush so the wood grain would show up well. He delivered the shoes by bicycle with a big bamboo basket to hold them.

My father had such a good heart. Some of the customers would come to buy shoes and he would let them pay later because they were poor. Sometimes, after I came home from school, my father would send me out to collect money. I hated this job. If the people said they didn't have any money, I had to go back another day to ask. If they still did not have money, then my father would say to me, "Never mind, they're so poor and have a bunch of kids. Let it go." My mother would be mad and say, "You are too kind to people. If a beggar came to the door, you'd offer him tea."

When neighbors needed noodles for the special wedding traditions, they would ask my father to make them. He was well-known for making good home-made Japanese noodles. Long narrow noodles mean long marriage life.

My father had a big board the size of a small table that he put on the floor to set the dough on. He covered the dough with two or three layers of some bleached muslin cloth and then he would walk on the covered dough in his bare feet to knead it. If he was making lots of dough, he would ask me to get on his shoulders to make more weight to knead it better. This was when I was about four or five years old. I had to be careful not to cover his eyes while I was holding on. Sometimes for fun he would twirl around to make me dizzy.

In the winter, the house was very cold in the morning because there was no heating. My father would get up early to start a fire to warm the house. He would make a wood and charcoal fire in the clay cooking stove. He would put some of the hot embers in a little hibachi grill and add charcoal to make another fire for cooking.

My father would also put some warm embers into a metal compartment at the bottom of a pit in the floor. We would put a low table across the pit and lay a quilt over that, like a tent, to keep the warm air from escaping out into the room. Then we would sit on floor cushions, with our legs down in the pit, and lay the edge of the quilt over our laps. This was our "kotatsu," or "foot-warmer."

My mother would get up at six o-clock each morning to make the breakfast. She would cook a big pot of rice on top of the clay stove and use the hibachi to cook "miso" soybean soup with a little bit of spinach or maybe a poached egg, and then make hot water for tea. There would be fish or vegetable for breakfast, too.

In the winter, my father would offer to cook breakfast. He would say to my mother, "It's no use for two of us to get up in a cold house, so I will make breakfast today and call you when it is ready." In those days, it was unusual for a Japanese man to help with cooking. Sometimes my mother would get up and cook anyway because she felt guilty staying in bed while her husband did women's work.

We didn't eat much meat. Most of the time we had vegetables, miso soup, and rice or noodles for every meal. Sometimes we had fish. We liked rice very much. We ate short-grain Japanese rice. It is a little sticky. Even today I only like to eat this kind of rice.

When I was growing up I did not drink milk, only green tea. The milkman would come by every day, but only a few neighbors would buy a small bottle, about a pint-size. My mother did not like the taste of milk, so we didn't buy any. I did not like milk either. Japanese children drink more milk these days; maybe that is why they grow taller now.

My mother did not eat meat, not even fish. She loved all kinds of fresh vegetables and fruit. She went to the butcher shop one time and saw a cow hanging upside down. She went home and was sick.

Still, my mother did cook meat just to please my father. She was a good cook and she always cooked what he liked. She would say to me, "Be good to your husband when you get married. Your husband brings food to your family."

My mother loved to eat pumpkins. Japanese pumpkins are green and are much smaller than the American ones for Halloween. They taste more like a sweet potato. In Japan, they are skinned, cut into pieces, and cooked with a little sugar and soy sauce. At dinnertime one day, my father said to my mother for a joke, "You eat too much pumpkin. Your face is becoming like a pumpkin. Look, Yaeko, her cheeks are round like a pumpkin!" My mother got mad.

For the evening meal, my mother liked to use nice plates and she would say to me, "A good chef makes food appetizing to your eyes before your stomach." She always decorated the food with garnishes. Sometimes she used leaves, or onions cut like flowers. She liked for the table to look pretty. Since she used pretty dishes, she would not let me wash them because she was afraid I might break one. That made me very happy not to wash dinner dishes.

In Japan it is very important to have good manners. One day my mother and I were going to visit her sister. On the way to her house my mother said to me, "When we get there, don't forget to bow to your aunt and say to her, 'Good afternoon.' That is good manners."

Japanese children had respect for parents and other adults and did not talk back. When I was growing up, I did not talk back to my mother, whether she was right or wrong. If I said anything bad, my mother would cry.

My mother taught me many things about what to do and not to do, and she had many wise sayings. I still remember some of them and tell them to my daughters. "Watch your tongue, what words you say cannot be put back in your mouth." She told me Aesop's fables and other moral stories and sayings that we called "shushin." She also taught me how to do things correctly. The first thing every morning when we cleaned the house, she would say, "When you sweep, sweep like the shape." In other words, don't skip the corners.

My mother sewed all our clothes. She could make silk kimonos, too, and would make them on order for other people. The sewing was done by hand-stitching with silk thread. The kimonos were beautiful and expensive. She used to say to me, "When you do your job, do it well because people see your character by your work."

It takes much patience and skill to do the hand-sewing for silk kimonos. Not many people can do it. My mother went to a sewing class for only eleven days and learned everything she wanted. She had a natural talent for sewing. I think I took after her that way.

I had pneumonia when I was about four months old. The doctor couldn't help me. My mother said that she took care of me day and night and hardly slept for three days. She put a moist towel on my chest and set a pan of hot water next to me and made a tent over me with a sheet. The tent helped to keep the moisture in to make it easier for me to breathe. Finally, I got better. The doctor said that only a mother's love and care saved me.

My mother was a very small woman, but she was strong and healthy and never got sick all her life. She did not even know what a headache was. She had no sympathy for other people's aches because she never had any herself. She never went to a doctor and was never in a hospital. She had a midwife to deliver her babies at home.

My mother lived to be in her eighties with no health problems. She did have a lot of trouble remembering things when she got old and even had to give up sewing. She grew tired of life. She began to sleep a lot. Toward the end, she was awake one day, only long enough to see her family gather around her for the last time. In Japan, it is called "the last blossoming." Then she just faded away.

My mother had a brother who lived nearby. My cousins were older so I didn't play with them, but sometimes I would walk to my uncle's house and visit him in his bakery. I liked to watch how he made the candies and cakes and other Japanese goodies. He made them all by hand. He would let me eat the ones that didn't turn out perfect. Once in awhile I would get a whole batch of hard candies to take home if they didn't turn out right. Mostly we did not have desserts, only fruit, so sweets were a real treat.

I have two older sisters and one younger brother. I hardly remember playing with my sisters because they were much older than me (they were four and seven years older). Also, because we were poor, when they were old enough my mother sent them to rich families to be maids or baby-sitters. My mother thought they would have a better life that way with good food to eat. Our country was in a deep depression in the 1930's so many people were poor.

I have some childhood memories of my middle sister, Iwa, but only one memory of my oldest sister, Ine. When I was about three years old, my mother scolded me and I cried and cried. Ine picked me up and carried me on her back to the steps of a nearby ice warehouse. She was singing a Japanese fairy tale song to me about angels in the sky. I fell asleep on her back.

When I was a small child, my little brother and I always played together. If he climbed a tree, I climbed, too. If he played with a kite, I played with a kite. Our father made the kites from wood scraps and paper. He also made adjustable stilts for us. My brother would walk with the stilts at the lowest setting and I would do the same. He would raise his setting and walk and so would I. I was a tomboy.

When my brother was seven, he got a bicycle with training wheels. I was jealous. I used to sneak and ride it and I got pretty good at it. One day my father removed the training wheels. I got on the bike and rode downhill on the little path behind our house that went across the stream. I lost control and fell into the water. The front end of the bike was all twisted and I had a cut on my knee. I sat in the stream crying for help. A man passing by helped me out and took me home.

My brother and my mother were so mad at me for taking the bike. Only my father felt sorry for me. I could not go outside for the next two days for my punishment. I have a scar on my knee to this day.

My mother would dress me so pretty in kimonos. Over the kimono I wore a white apron with lace edges and a big bow in the back. We did not have western clothes when I was very young. Girls wore informal knee-length cotton kimonos.

My mother put nice clothes on me and expected me to stay clean all day, but when I played with my brother that was impossible. One day my brother and I found ripe mulberries growing all over in the nearby field. We ate them and our tongues turned blue. I put mulberries in my white apron pocket. Then my brother took me to a nearby shrine where there was a tree with branches perfect to jump on and climb. I jumped on a branch. I was doing somer-saults around the tree branch and smashed all the mulberries in my pocket.

My mother was very upset about the dark purple mulberry stain on my white apron. She said, "You are a girl. Can't you behave? Why don't you act like a young lady?" She put ashes in the water to soak the apron and then rubbed out the stain. We did not have bleach in those days.

One day when I was about five years old, a neighbor girl who was three years older than me asked me to go to a nearby park with her. I was so excited to go to that park. I had never been there before. My mother had told me, "Wherever you go, you must tell me," but I forgot to tell my mother where I was going and I went with the neighbor girl to the park.

The park was on top of a steep hill. We climbed the stairs and saw there were a lot of boys and girls playing, but they were all older than me. I thought I would have fun, but I didn't because no one would pay attention to me. I told the neighbor girl that I wanted to go home. She said, "Okay, I will see you later."

I climbed down the long stairway to the street and could not remember how to get home. I began to cry. There was an older lady passing by. She asked me why I was crying. I told her, "I don't know the way home. Please tell me the way home." She said to me, "Young girl, if you don't know, I don't know either." That made me cry harder. She asked me what my father's name was. I said, "I don't know...just Father." She asked me what he did. I said he was a shoemaker. Then the woman said to me, "Oh, I know who you belong to! Follow me." She took me to my house.

When I saw my mother, I was scared and I did not tell her where I had been. She didn't scold me. She said to me, "Open your hands." Then she gave to me three sen (like American pennies) and said, "Now stop crying." My mother knew the woman who took me home. She would come down the street early every other morning selling fresh eggs and my mother would buy some from her. After that, I never forgot to tell my mother where I was going.

I was happy to have the three sen. The first sen I spent next door at the grocery shop. I bought a small box of candy. The second sen I spent when a man came by on a bicycle with a megaphone calling, "Hot wheat buns!" We did not have ovens, so it was a treat to get baked bread.

The third sen I spent on the storyteller. Every afternoon the storyteller came by on his bicycle. For one sen he would give you a lollipop and let you see a show. On the back of his bicycle, he had a plywood box with an opening cut in it. He put big slides of Betty Boop or other cartoons in the opening and he would tell the story. He also told a special children's story. When the story got exciting, he would beat his drum. Then he would say, "See you tomorrow, same time!" We looked forward to the next day and the exciting stories of the "kamishibai" man.

Sometimes a candyman would come to town. He would beat on a drum to let us know he was coming. For one sen he would make an animal shape out of a kind of boiled syrup. He would take a bit of the warm, very soft dough from a heated container and put it on the end of a stick and twirl it up and down and around to keep it from dripping. All the while he would pull and cut to make the shape of a fish or bird or animal. To puff up the body, he would use a straw to blow into the shape. He would do all this very fast, before the dough hardened. This is called "amezaiku." After the sugar mix cooled it became candy on a stick. Sometimes the candyman would paint his creation with food coloring or dye to make a yellow horse or a red dragon or other colorful creature.

When I was about seven years old, new neighbors moved nearby. They had eight children in a small house. I found a friend. She was one year older than me and had the same name as me. So I stopped playing with my brother so much and started playing with her.

I remember one time when my mother gave me "Boys' Day" food. Boys' Day, or "Tangu no Sekku" is a day in May to celebrate boy children. Now it is also called "Children's Day." The special food for Boys' Day is sweet red bean paste put inside folded rice cakes. An oak leaf is wrapped around the outside and the pastry is steamed. I didn't care for red bean paste so I took the inside paste, rolled it up like a ball, and threw it away to the rooftop. I hoped it would go in the gutter so my mother wouldn't know what I did. My neighbor girlfriend thought that was so funny, but it wasn't funny to me because when I did wrong things I felt bad. My mother always said to me, "Don't throw away good food. We have a shortage of food."

Japanese people have special days to celebrate boys and girls. On Boys' Day, which is May fifth, warrior dolls are displayed and families go to a shrine so the priest can pray to the gods for strength and success for the boys. Families put a long bamboo pole on their balcony or roof. At the very top of the pole is a pinwheel and sometimes streamers. On the pole are windsocks of big carp, one for every boy in the family. The families go to the shrines to pray and hope the boys will grow up brave and strong like the carp, which can fight the river currents to swim upstream. It is a pretty view—long, colorful windsocks in the sky and a gentle breeze making them float in the air.

March third is the Girls' Day Festival, or "Hina Matsuri." It is when the peach trees blossom and is a celebration of springtime and young girls. Some people call it "Dolls' Day." Parents of girls display beautiful old-style dolls dressed in the traditional costumes of the emperor's court. The porcelain dolls "celebrate" with the family. Mothers make rice cakes to offer to the dolls, wishing young girls to grow up as elegant as the dolls. The family goes to a shrine to pray and the priest asks for blessings for the girls.

My mother made "sekihan," which is sticky rice mixed with sweet red beans that would color the rice pink. She also made "mochi" rice cakes that were colored pink. Rice cakes are made of the special sticky rice, cooked and pounded into a paste and shaped into small thick patties. Sometimes we put them in soup. Sometimes we grilled the cakes to make them warm and soften them. Then we dipped them in soy sauce and wrapped each with a piece of dried seaweed.

My new neighbor friend and I liked to play house. We spread a straw mat in the yard. We took our shoes off to go in, just like we did in our real houses. We made "dinner" of flower petal soup and mud pancakes. We used the white rinse water from washing rice grains as our milk and squeezed purple morning glory flowers in water to make our juice. Sometimes we mashed four-o'clock flower seeds to make a white powder that we used on our faces for makeup.

My mother sometimes would make us snacks of steamed chestnuts or baked yam (sweet potato). One day my friend said, "Who is brave enough to smash the yam with their bare foot?" I said, "I am!" So I did, and my foot was burned so badly from the hot potato that I jumped up and down crying in pain. My mother put ointment on the bottom of my foot and scolded me, "Yai-chan, you can listen to friends, but use common sense."

There was a geisha house a few blocks away from where I lived. Sometimes when my friend and I would go near it, we would hear singing coming from the house, in the strange voice of the traditional Japanese way. Sometimes there was the sound of someone playing a string instrument. Sometimes we could hear laughing and party sounds in the evening. We could not see much of the house from the street because of the walled garden and trees, but we wished we could peep in the windows to see what was going on.

Every once in awhile we would see pretty geisha girls walking carefully down the street in beautiful, long-sleeve silk kimonos and hair fixed high on their heads with fancy comb decorations. They wore heavy white makeup on their faces and necks and had tiny red-painted lips. We would stop and watch them, but tried not to stare because that was not polite. They were very high class girls, very proper. At New Year's the geisha would walk down the street in a line on their way to a shrine perhaps. That was a beautiful sight to see.

I had other friends I could play with, too. We always played outside. We would go down to the creek to find tadpoles or tree snails with shells that were a beautiful shining white, like mother-of-pearl. Sometimes we made origami paper boats and went to the creek to let them go to see whose boat would go the fastest. We would run along the creek to watch the boats as they floated with the current. Sometimes we made boats from bamboo leaves and put ants inside to ride them. We didn't have many toys, but we didn't know we were missing anything. We were very happy children.

My mother liked nature and would take us out to play sometimes. I remember going with her and my brother and my middle sister to the rice paddies. The rice paddies were flooded with shallow water and we would look for tadpoles, crawfish, and snails among the grassy rice plants near the water edge. We loved this. We would take jars to bring the tadpoles home in, but we let the crawfish go. When the tadpoles grew legs, we would take them back to the paddies. My mother would bring home some of the chives growing along the paddies. Sometimes we would take a sack lunch and rice bowls and we would eat in the fields.

My mother told us not to reach too far into the rice paddies or we would sink into the mud. Once my sister tried to reach a snail and her hand went down into the watery mud. Her arm sank deep, almost to her shoulder, and she screamed with fear. My mother rushed over and pulled her out by her "obi," which is the kimono sash.

Japanese people enjoy nature and celebrate it with some special traditions. One tradition is to welcome the spring by having a picnic under the cherry blossoms, or "sakura." The Cherry Blossom Festival is also called "Hanami," which means the "flower-viewing." The blossoms last only a short time before the petals fall away like snow, reminding us of how beautiful and short our lives are.

Sometimes my mother took me to a park in our town during the cherry blossom festival time. It was crowded with people who were eating and drinking and laughing. We brought our own food, but there were booths set up at the park that sold food and goodies. In the evening there would be folk dances.

Another nature celebration is the "Full Moon-Viewing," or "Tsukimi," in September. My mother and I went to the fields to gather seven or fifteen stalks of "shear" grass, like pampas grass, and seven stems of fall wildflowers to make a flower arrangement. Seven and fifteen were the lucky numbers. We celebrated the harvest moon by finding many round things to offer to the moon. My mother made rice-flour dumplings and bought grapes, persimmons, Asian pears, or any kind of round food to set on a pretty plate. We enjoyed celebrating the beauty of the moon by sitting outside in the evening, relaxing and watching the big moon.

When I was a little girl my mother said to me, "Look at the moon. There is a dark shadow on it. That is Rabbit pounding rice with a big wooden hammer to make mochi rice cakes." That is part of a Japanese fairy tale. I used to believe it.

We used to celebrate a fairy tale story. July seventh is the "Stars Festival," or "Love Night." It is not celebrated so much these days, but we used to enjoy the summer evenings of stars with a romantic story.

On the west side of the Milky Way there is a herd boy, and on the east side there is a princess. Each year on the seventh day of the seventh month, the King of the Sky lets his daughter cross over the Milky Way to meet the herd boy. Some people call this the "Festival of the Weaver" because the women hope to become good weavers, making the best of cloth like the princess, who is a good weaver and makes the delicate clouds and mist.

For the Stars Festival, my father would bring home a cut bamboo tree. We used colorful paper to make paper chains and folded origami birds. We also made "kirigami," which is colored paper folded and cut to open into pretty shapes. We also cut paper strips about 3 x 7 inches, and whatever we wished for we wrote down in black ink with a brush, or we just wrote "Tanabata," which is another name for the Stars Festival. All those things were tied onto the branches. Then my father set up the bamboo tree outside by the house.

The trees remind the King of the Sky of his promise to let the princess see the herd boy. Every house of the town was decorated with bamboo trees full of colorful paper. The tall thin trees had so many decorations that they bent over to make arches across the streets. It was such a pretty sight on a summer evening.

One year, my family went to see a big Tanabata festival with fireworks. My mother put on me a white cotton summer kimono with a design of big pink hydrangea flowers. It was my sister's, second-hand, but it was very pretty. I spent one sen on cotton candy. Another sen I used at a booth to catch goldfish with a paper net. I had to be quick to catch one before the net melted into the water. That time I was lucky and caught two goldfish!

We didn't have many toys except what we made from nature. I did have one little porcelain doll with moveable arms and legs and eyes that opened and closed. The doll got so worn that the hair came off. I glued embroidery thread on her head for hair. Her name was Hanako, which means "flower child." My mother would get upset that I played with her so much instead of helping with house work.

I used to sit beside my mother when she was sewing and learned to sew by hand by watching her. I started making doll clothes. I made a blue pleated skirt and a white sailor top with a tie in the front. My mother was amazed at how creative I was because even she didn't know how to make western clothes. My doll looked so happy in her pretty new outfit. I made pajamas for her and slept with her. I made a cardboard dollhouse, too. I still love dolls.

When I was about eleven or twelve years old, I learned all by myself how to make my own little dolls from cloth. They were very small, about four inches tall. I glued them onto little wooden stands.

One I made with winter clothes and snow skis; another was a geisha with a parasol. I used smashed rice to glue black embroidery thread on their heads for hair. I gave most of the dolls away to my friends, but I still have a few. My daughters are amazed at how I could make such delicate, pretty dolls when I was so young.

I loved my mother, but I felt her love was unfair —that she loved my brother more than me. She would take my brother's side, right or wrong. She always corrected me. My mother would say that girls are not so good to have because they marry and leave home, but when a son gets married, he stays to take care of his parents. It was Japanese custom that the oldest boy was to take care of his parents in their old age.

My parents had only one son so I guess my mother felt that she should always be nice to him so that he would grow up and want to care for his parents. I thought my brother was a spoiled brat because he was never corrected. When he got older, he mistreated my mother and me and still she did not correct him.

Sometimes I was jealous when my mother didn't give me the same amount of love as my brother. On Mother's Day one year when I was older, I gave my mother a bouquet of flowers and a small box of candy. She said, "I got flowers from my son. I don't think I need more. You can take them to someone else you know." I am very sensitive so I was very hurt. I hoped that some day if I had my own children, I would love them equal.

I think my father saw that my mother loved my brother more, and so he gave his affection mostly to me. My father was a busy man, but he would often make time to spend with me. Sometimes, a few days after a soft rain, he would ask me if I wanted to go mushroom hunting with him. He knew all about what was good to eat and what was not. He would take a small bag and we would go looking in the woods. Different kinds of mushrooms grew under different kinds of trees.

One time, when I was busy looking for mushrooms I looked up and my hair touched a huge spider web stretching between two trees. There was a big spider in the middle of the web! I was so scared and I screamed so loud. My father said, "Don't go forward, back up!" I will never forget what a big spider was so close to my face.

Another day we went mushroom hunting but couldn't find any. My father saw a baby owl sleeping on a pine branch. He said, "Do you want an owl for a pet?" He put it in the bag and took it home. My mother put it in a birdcage. We fed it insects and worms. The owl grew up and started hooting at night. My father said, "We have to let it go. It needs freedom and a friend." So we let the owl go free.

The owl did not go too far from our house. It stayed in a big elm tree and made lots of noise at night. We wished it would go farther away! Within a year it disappeared and we hoped that it found happiness.

Sometimes on summer evenings, my father would ask me if I wanted to catch lightning bugs with him. Japanese lightning bugs stay lighted and do not blink. We had a net to catch them. One time, as it was getting dark, my father was crossing the old wooden bridge over the creek and stepped on a rotting board. His leg fell through and I was so scared that I screamed, "Dear Father, please don't get hurt!" Fortunately, he was all right.

We would put the lightning bugs in an insect cage. Japanese insect cages are made of bamboo and it takes hours and hours to make the many fine details. I still have one that looks like a little house with sliding screen doors and a tiny bench.

On summer days, a peddler on a three-wheeled bicycle came selling beautiful homemade insect cages in all kinds of shapes. The peddler also sold little black "bell-ring" insects that made a sound like a soft bell ringing at night. He also sold bigger insects that looked like green crickets and made a sound like "sweet sweet tch-tch-tch". We fed the insects slices of cucumber or watermelon.

Every year in the winter season in my hometown area there is a strong, dry wind blowing at night from the Chichibu mountain range. Our area is known for the wind. Our town hired men to watch out at night for fires in the dry season. They walked around in town with wooden claps. Each hour they would strike the wooden blocks together to tell us what time it was. If the time was three o-clock, the men struck their blocks three times. They watched the town to be sure no fires started by accident. Our houses were made of wood and we used wood and charcoal fires to keep warm and to cook meals, so sometimes the wind would blow the hot ash and cause a fire to start.

If the wind was strong in the daytime, too, men watched all day for fire. They had long metal sticks with the top part having about five metal rings on it. They hit the ground with the sticks, then the rings at the top hit together to make noise. They came every hour just like the night watchmen. They bundled up with heavy clothes, scarves and knitted caps with coverings for their faces.

One day, my neighbor friend and I followed a watchman. It was such a cold, windy day. We pretended we were fire-watchers. The watchman stopped at his shed where he had a little homemade stove that was nice and hot to warm him up. He made us each a baked yam. My friend and I kept him company for awhile. We thought that was fun to be his helpers.

One Sunday morning, a friend across the street asked me to go to Sunday school. I asked her what it was. She said, "They give you a coloring book of baby Jesus and we sing songs." So I went with her. We had to walk half an hour to get there, so we only went a few times and didn't learn much.

Many people in Japan practice Shinto. Shinto shrines are in every town and many have the red "torii" gate at the entrance. I never learned much about Japanese religions except to know that they are very old traditions. Shinto believes in many gods and spirits. We went to Shinto shrines to pray to the gods for blessings and happiness especially on occasions like New Year's Day or for weddings or to celebrate new babies. We would wear fancy kimonos, put money in the donation box at the shrine, and pull the rope to ring the bell that called the spirits. Then we would pray. At the special ceremonies the priest would pray for blessings.

The New Year holiday, called "Shogatsu," is the biggest celebration in Japan. It is a three-day festival. When I was young, everyone became one year older on New Year's Day, so we didn't celebrate our real birthdays.

On New Year's Day almost everyone goes to the Shinto shrines to pray to the gods for best wishes and good health for the coming year and to throw coins in the offering box. People go to the shrines anytime from very early in the morning to the end of the day.

My family would go to the shrine right after midnight. We all wore our nicest clothes. My mother would put a pretty kimono on me that once belonged to my sister and I would get new shoes from my father. Over the top of my winter kimono I wore a "haori." It is like a short quilted coat.

Outside the shrine entrance, there were all kinds of booths selling special festival food, toys, candy, and good-luck charms. My mother would give me some spending money and I would buy a Kewpie doll or some candy.

My mother would clean the house and make fresh beds before the New Year to get rid of old dirt and be ready for a new start. She cooked special food for the New Year. The night before, we would have buckwheat soba noodles that are long and narrow and would bring wishes for long life. On New Year's Day we had mochi rice cakes for good luck. Even now in America, I eat mochi every New Year's Day.

My mother offered food and tea to everyone who came to visit. My aunt and uncle would bring their family to see us. My two sisters also would come home. I never did see my father's side of the family. They lived far away and could not visit us.

In the evening we played a traditional New Year card game that is called "karuta." Picture cards were placed facing up, and my father read cards with wise sayings like "People can't change truth, but truth can change people." We would try to be the first one to grab the picture card that matched what he had said. The picture cards had some writing on them to help with the matching.

Another old Shinto tradition is "Setsubun." This is a special day in February, on the last day of winter. It is a day to chase away evil spirits. My father would stand at the door and throw roasted soybeans into the house, saying in a loud voice, "Happiness in!" Then he would shut the door, saying, "Evil out!" We could also go to a shrine and the priest would throw the beans to chase away evil.

Many towns would have parades for their local Shinto god. Strong men would carry on their shoulders a heavy wooden platform that held the shrine for the god. It was believed that the god's spirit was in the shrine. Sometimes the men would dance and jump very wild with the "omikoshi" and that made the parade very fun to watch.

Japanese people also practice Buddhist religion. It is often mixed with Shinto traditions. Shinto is a way of living that respects nature, and Buddhism is the way of belief for after life.

Most cemeteries are near a Buddhist temple because people go to the temples for funerals and at other times to pray for souls to rest in peace in the Buddhist tradition. They bring fresh flowers to the graves to comfort the dead souls of their relatives. They sprinkle water and rice grains over the graves to feed the souls.

The Obon Festival is an important Buddhist celebration for the dead and is for paying respect to ancestors. It is still celebrated today in Japan. It is three days in mid-July or mid-August, depending on what part of the country you live in.

In my hometown, Obon was in August. All the families took lanterns to the cemetery and prayed for their ancestors' souls. We burned incense to help the dead souls find their way back to us. The souls were invited into the lanterns and the candles inside were lit. Then the souls were carried back to the homes.

At the home, the burning candle was taken out of the lantern and put in a small Buddhist altar in the house. Families prayed for the souls, and favorite foods of the dead relatives were offered to the souls. Every morning while our ancestors were visiting, my mother burned incense and put a small bowl of cooked rice and a cup of green tea in front of the candle. She prayed for the souls, to welcome them back to the home and hope that peace would be in their hearts. After visiting with the family for two days, the souls have to go back to the world of the dead. In the evening, the lighted candle was set inside a square wood-framed lantern of white rice paper, and the lantern was put into the river, floating on a piece of wood. It was so pretty to see the reflection of the lights and the many lanterns bobbing on the water.

Special towers were set up and decorated with big colorful hanging paper lanterns, and festival music was played through speakers. Men played big "taiko" drums. People wore casual, light-weight cotton summer kimonos, called "yukata," with fans tucked into their obi sashes. We danced "Bon-odori" folk dances around the towers all evening. I remember taking lessons for two weeks to learn some of the Obon dances. It was so much fun at the Obon Festivals.

In our country in the old days, sometimes you would see in wooded areas or in someone's garden a small shrine with a little white fox statue. Some people, especially merchants, sacrificed food offerings to the fox. Some shop-owners would keep a little fox statue on their shelves for good luck and success in business. This was part of a Shinto belief in animals with magic powers.

My mother would tell us "Old Fox" stories. One summer day, my mother said, "What a beautiful day it is! Children, would you like to go on a picnic today?" My mother made lunch for us to take. We went through the woods and saw a dead cat hanging on a tree branch. We were scared and screamed! My sister said, "I wonder who does such mischief like that?" My mother said, "Maybe the Old Fox did that. Do you know that the Old Fox fools people? If you go through the woods alone, it is best to sing a song in a loud voice, or if men go through smoking tobacco, then the Old Fox doesn't come nearby. He is invisible and you can not see him."

One afternoon my brother and his friend rode their bicycles to go fishing. They went to the fishing spot often and knew how to get there and come back home, but that day something strange happened. My brother had not come home and it was close to evening. The neighbor boy had come home early because he didn't catch any fish. My father worried about my brother and asked the neighbor about him. He did not know where my brother was.

My father went in the woods. He saw my brother's bicycle, but not him. My father searched and searched and finally did find him. My brother was so dirty. He said he got lost and walked around in circles many times and he was tired. My mother said, "I bet the Old Fox fooled him."

I wasn't sure whether to believe the Fox stories, but in Japan in the countryside, older people talked about things like that. It was a hot summer evening story, the kind to tell when we sat outside to catch the cool breeze and the older people told scary stories about Old Foxes and weasels and ghosts.

My father told us that when he was young and lived on a big farm, he saw lights blinking like lanterns in a field and heard noises far away, like people speaking a strange language. He went outside to the field, but nothing was there. He told his parents and they said, "Oh, that is the Old Fox's wedding. You can't see it because it is invisible."

My mother told us a story about one night when she was sixteen years old and was in the house weaving material for kimonos. It was the fall season and the tree leaves were rustling and acorns fell loud on the tin roof. She heard knocking at the door, so she opened the door, but no one was there. It happened again. My mother said it was a bad weasel hitting his tail against the door to fool her. She would tell me that certain old animals would try to fool people and I should be careful of them.

On summer evenings we used to play a fun game that we called "summertime adventure," or "courage test." We drew a big circle in the dirt and divided it into four or five sections. Each section had writing for where to go and what to do. We took turns throwing a stone into the circle to see what task we had to do. The directions were things like go to the graveyard and bring back leaves of a certain tree. Then, on the way to the cemetery one of the other children would hide behind a bush and make strange, spooky noises like a ghost. If we did not get the tree leaf to prove we went there, then we lost the game.

Once when it was my turn, I had to go to the ice warehouse and get a handful of the straw that was used to help keep the ice blocks from melting. The small warehouse was by our neighbor's house. I took a flashlight so I could see better. When I got inside, I saw legs of a man hanging from a log rafter close to the ceiling. I was scared and screamed and ran away, and I did lose the game.

We also would play hide-and-seek with partners. Once, a few of us hid inside a big sake wine barrel set out to dry. The owner came and chased us away with a broom and so we were found and lost the game.

I had a very happy childhood. I have so many good memories...

School

In April, 1932, I went to school for the first time. A long time ago, there was no kindergarten. Children started to school at seven or eight years of age. Our town had only one school. Each grade level had three or four classes with about thirty children in each class. Boys were in a separate building from the girls.

For my very first day of school, my mother gave me a new western-style dress and new blue tennis shoes to wear. That was a very special treat for me because most of the time my mother put on me my sister's secondhand clothes—and, that was the first time I had an American-style dress! The dress was a wine-red jumper with a white blouse.

I was very happy and excited and took the dress to my bed and slept with it. I told my mother, "I promise I'll take good care of my new dress and keep it clean until Sunday." In other words, I would wear the same clothes for six days, and Sunday my mother could wash them so I could wear them to school again on Monday. She said, "White blouse to wear for six days? I don't think so." But I didn't want to wear a kimono anymore. I loved the dress!

On the first day of school, my father wrote a little note and put it on the back of my closet door. It said "right, straight, honest and cheerful." These words my mother always said to me, not my father! But he said, "Yaeko, every morning before you change clothes, look at these words, then be cheerful and show to your friends kindness of heart. I know you can do it. If you do this, it will show outside of you. Just remember that."

Then my father said, "I'll take you to school and show you the way to go." He asked a neighbor girlfriend to come with us. It took almost twenty-five minutes to walk to school. My father was very nice—if it rained on a school day, he came to the school and brought an umbrella for me.

At school, all the children took their shoes off and changed into slippers. There were rows of wooden boxes near the entrance to the classroom and everyone put their shoes in the boxes. Each box had a student's name on it. In the corner of the room we had a wood-burning stove, but in the winter the room still was not so warm. Everyone brought their own box lunch with rice and cooked vegetables, cooked fish or some other meat, and apple or mandarin orange.

Children must respect their teacher. When our teacher came in our classroom, we all bowed to her and said, "Sensei, ohayo gozaimasu," which means "Good morning, Teacher." If I ever saw our teacher outside of school I bowed and said, "Konnichi wa," which means "good day." I remember how my first teacher was kind and nice. I liked her very much.

When we first got to school we went to the janitor's room. The janitor gave us buckets of water from the well to use to clean our classrooms. In the winter he heated the water over a charcoal fire so it wouldn't be too cold for us. Everyone in class helped clean the room. We cleaned the blackboards and dusted. We also scrubbed the wooden floors and hallways with rags. The janitor cleaned the bathrooms, the gym floor, and the windows.

Next we had to go in the schoolyard for exercise hour. Organ music played across a speaker to give us music to exercise to. We did reaching, bending, and twisting in time with the music.

Then we went inside to study. There was no recess time, just lots of studying. Every weekday we stayed at school eight hours, and on Saturday we stayed five hours. Even on Sundays we still had our homework to do.

Our summer vacation was just one month— August—but we had workbooks that we had to take home and do lessons in every day. There was reading, math and geography. Once a week we had to take the workbooks to school to be graded and stamped. If the grades weren't good, we had to do the work all over again. The teachers also gave you a subject that you liked to do, like sewing or sketching, and that had to be taken for grading. As we got older there were summer projects like sewing for girls or wood crafts for boys. Once we had to collect insects and identify them.

One summer vacation our teacher volunteered for the girls to sweep the garden at the neighborhood shrine. I didn't like to get up at six o-clock in the morning during the vacation time, but my mother woke me and I had to go because the teacher was waiting at the shrine. She would stamp our hands for attendance so we couldn't cheat and stay home. Fortunately we were assigned to do this only a few times.

In the second grade, we had a big blackboard covering a whole wall in our classroom. The teacher asked me to take colored chalk and each season draw a picture on the board to represent that season. I remember one time drawing some girls that were wearing fancy kimonos and playing a New Year's game that is like badminton. Everyone else would go home, but I had to stay and draw the pictures on the blackboard.

The teacher thought I had talent in art, but I didn't like having to stay after school to draw. The first time I had to stay late the teacher saw tears on my face and asked me why I was crying. I told her I wanted to go home and play like everyone else. She said, "Oh, my dear, you have a gift that you should share with others!" I didn't care, I just wanted to go home.

In school we had lessons in morals, like the Aesop's story of the boy who cried wolf for a joke, and when a real wolf came no one listened. Most of our reading was Aesop's fables or other "shushin" moral stories and sayings that taught us how to behave properly.

One day the teacher taught us how to write "haiku" poetry. She told us first we must get close to nature, to hear or see things, and then find the feeling inside ourselves. She took us to the woods and said, "Now we are in the very quiet woods and you must listen carefully." There I felt a gentle breeze shaking the treetops and heard a little insect singing. Those sounds and feelings make haiku poetry. I used to love writing the poems.

In third grade, we had a class in crafts. We made crepe paper flowers, pin cushions, tie-dyed scarves, and other things. In the older grades we had crafts lessons, too. That was my favorite subject in school.

In the fourth grade, we learned penmanship. We each had a paintbrush and a small black tile with a block of dry black ink on it. We added a little water to the blocks and brushed back and forth to dissolve the hard ink. Then we were taught how to take the brush and write artistic letters on thin rice paper.

Learning to write Japanese takes a long time. There are two kinds of alphabets. The "hiragana" has forty-eight symbols that mean simple sounds, like "ka" or "ke." The other kind of alphabet is Chinese character symbols, called "kanji." Each kanji means a whole word or idea, like "mountain" or "peace." There are thousands of Chinese kanji to learn, but children learn just basic characters in primary school. There are much more to learn after that. There is also the "katakana" that has simple characters that are special sounds to help write foreign words, like "dress" or "ice cream" in our language. Writing is very difficult to learn in Japan.

That year in fourth grade we had an exchange with students in Holland. My teacher asked me to stay after school to draw pictures to send to Holland. I didn't want to, but I could not say no to the teacher. The students in Holland sent their pictures to our school, too, and in a long hallway all kinds of pictures were displayed.

In the fifth grade, the girls were taught how to make their own clothes. The school had sewing machines for us to use. We bought material from a peddler. I made a dress with a lace collar, and also a slip to wear with it. By this time most of the children were wearing western-style clothes like the ones from Europe and America every day.

In sixth grade, I made a kimono of cotton material. Kimonos were hand-stitched and it was very difficult to do. My mother would watch me work on the kimono at home and tell me to make my stitches smaller.

We had weekly art class in the older grades. The teacher would take us outside and we would sketch the scenery. Sometimes in the classroom there would be on the table a vase of flowers for us to draw. In sixth grade we began to use watercolors to learn painting.

I always got good grades in art, but I didn't know where I got my talent from. My mother could sew very well, and my father could make shoes, but no one in my family could draw well and no one cared to make crafts. I just had a natural talent.

That year in sixth grade, I sent a care package to a Japanese soldier in Manchuria. Many children in the class volunteered to write to soldiers fighting in that part of China. We did not know what they were fighting for. I sent rice cracker snacks, gloves, and a hand-drawn picture. The soldier wrote to thank me for the picture and told me he liked it very much. He asked me to send more.

Several years later, the soldier came back to the homeland as a civilian. His mother said that he didn't come to see her, he came straight to see me— to see who it was that sent him the packages. He lived on a farm not too far away and came to visit me a few times.

One day my soldier friend asked me if I would like to see a movie with him. My mother said, "You're too young to go out with men. You should introduce him to your sister. She is older than you." I was not interested yet in going out with men anyway so my middle sister started dating him, and she ended up marrying him.

The highlights of school for me were crafts and sewing, but a highlight for everyone was picnic day in April or May. We took our lunches to a park or to the woods. The older students would stay overnight in a hotel. My parents wouldn't let me go to a hotel because we did not have enough money.

Sometimes we had field trips, too. One time we went to the silkworm farm. Another time we went to visit a tea factory to see how the tea leaves were dried in the sun and steamed.

I was graduated from school after sixth grade. A few years later, the school system changed so that primary school went to eighth grade. It was common for children, especially girls, from the poorer families not to take any more school than that.

I wanted to go to the secondary school, but my mother didn't think it was necessary for a woman to have education. She said that when a woman got married, her husband would not want her to be better educated than he was. All she needed to know was how to cook, keep house, and take care of children. My mother did not have much education. When she was young, children did not have to go to school. She chose to stop going after the third grade and worked as a babysitter to make money.

My parents could not afford for me to take more schooling anyway. This was the Depression and many people were poor. My mother would mend our socks by putting a light bulb in a sock while she stitched. She did a very neat job, but it was still embarrassing to me to wear mended socks to school. We had to take good care of our clothes so they would last a long time. The first couple years of school I tried to wear my western dress every day until it became too small for me, but my mother told me I had to wear a kimono sometimes. Later she did make a pleated skirt of deep purple wool for me by looking at how the jumper was made.

I liked to read books in bed at night, but my mother said not to waste electricity. She turned off the lights. I tried to read with a flashlight, but she did not like that either. Most of my books were shushin stories that taught moral lessons.

At mealtime we had only a small amount of food. There was a shortage of rice so we mixed chopped sweet potatoes into our rice so there would be more food to fill us up better. Sometimes we cooked wheat grains with our rice.

We had to eat everything my mother cooked if we liked it or not. My mother would not let us waste food. Even today I can't waste food. I scrape the jars and save all the leftovers, no matter how small. My children laugh, but I always remember the days when we were very poor. We were lucky that we always had a little food to eat every day.

My mother would go in the late spring to a tea field to work picking new tender leaves to get extra money for our family. The area around the nearby towns of Sayama and Iruma is known for good quality green tea. After the tea leaves are picked, they are separated into different grades. Bancha is the everyday tea. Sencha is better. There are very high quality expensive teas, too. The best tea comes from the fresh new growing tips of the bushes.

When I was in fifth grade, my mother asked me if I wanted to help in the tea field during a spring break from school so I could earn some money. We left very early in the morning and walked for a half hour to get to the field. There were acres of tea bushes and a lot of women were working in the field. We had big deep baskets to fill with new tea leaves. Midmorning, the owner's wife came to bring us tea and snacks. She also gave us tea to drink with the lunches we brought. It was hot so we wore straw hats with big brims to keep the sun off of our faces.

I didn't like picking the tea leaves. Tea bushes are short so it was not too hard to pick the leaves, even though we did have to stoop. It was hot and dull work. It was common for children to pick tea, but here there was no one else near my age to talk to. I only went for a few days and got just a little bit of money because I did not pick very fast like the adults and because my mother took most of the money I made. My fingers stayed green for several days after the picking.

My father was struggling because people weren't buying much. He had to lay off his one helper. My sisters were sent off to work for wealthy families after they finished grade school because my mother thought they would have better food. Their money was sent home to my parents.

When I finished the sixth grade at school, I had to go away to work. My parents kept my salary except for a small allowance for me. I lived with a grain merchant's family in my town, taking care of their little baby and helping with the housework.

I was homesick and cried at night so the family let me take the baby to visit my parents. I would put the baby on my back, wrap her tight to me with an obi sash and walk home for a visit. That was a common way to carry small children. I could not return home overnight except on holidays like New Year's Day or Obon. That was just the way it was in those days.

World War II
The End of Childhood

In 1939, we heard that war had started in Europe. Japan had been fighting in Manchuria for a long time and then in other parts of China. Now Japan became friendly with Germany and Italy. Those countries were attacking other European countries and Japan began to attack other Asian countries. The United States did not enter this big war until in December, 1941, after the Japanese warplanes made a surprise bombing attack on American warships in Pearl Harbor in Hawaii. I was sixteen years old then and too young to bother paying much attention to something far away. After Pearl Harbor, though, we began to listen to the radio to hear how many enemy ships sank, how many bombs were dropped, and how many airplanes were shot down. We celebrated when we heard our soldiers had won a battle. We never heard how many of our soldiers were killed or how much damage was done by the enemy.

Soon things got very bad. There was a shortage of food and fuel and many common goods. My mother began to be worried that maybe the government would draft women to go to dangerous areas to take care of wounded soldiers. She sent me to work for her friend in the town of Kamata on the edge of Tokyo. The friend's husband was a soldier. My mother said, "You must go there and help my friend. If you have a job with a soldier's wife, maybe you will be safe from drafting."

My father went with me on the train to go to Tokyo. He stayed overnight at the friend's house. The next day when he started home, I went with him to the train station. On the way he said, "Don't come all the way to the station. I want you to go back." I said goodbye to my father, and he said to me, "I will not look back to see you, so you go ahead and go straight back to the house." But he did look back at me. I was standing there with tears running down my face.

I was Father's girl. I would miss him so much. Every night for a long time the tears wet my pillow and I hoped he would come to me and take me back home. My mother told me later that my father said that was the hardest thing he ever had to do, to leave me in the city.

The separation was very sad. It was the first time I was far away from my family. I missed seeing Mt. Fuji in the distance, the mulberry bushes growing in the field, and the clear water of the stream. I was homesick.

I got a letter from my father a month later. He said he felt sorry that he left me in the big city of Tokyo. He missed me very much. He hoped that some day soon we would meet again. "My dear Yaeko, be patient. You're my big girl."

I kept that letter for a long time. I put it underneath my pillow and slept with it. Sometimes, when I couldn't sleep, I opened the letter and read it over again. The friend did not know how I felt. I hid from her my sadness.

I called the friend, "Auntie." She had a small grocery store. Her husband was drafted in the army and she did not know where he was for several years. I helped her in the shop. We thought I did not get drafted because I was helping a soldier's family, but I don't really think the government ever did draft girls.

Auntie and I worked hard—we were doing the job of men. Where were all the young men? They were all gone to be soldiers. We worked so hard sometimes that we were exhausted and tired to the bones, and I didn't care if I went to bed dirty. We had to walk to a warehouse to fill our big barrels and crates with food. On the way back I would pull our three-wheeled wooden wagon full of the heavy containers while Auntie pushed the back end. We had to struggle along the road for about an hour to get back home.

Things were getting worse every day. Everything was rationed. The government gave out coupons that told each family how much food or clothes they would get. We couldn't buy clothes or shoes or anything, only use the coupons. My job at the store was to measure out the food rations.

What good was it to have money if everything was rationed? But, you could trade or buy in secret on the black market. The butcher would bring meat to my aunt and exchange it for rice wine. Others would bring silk fabric and exchange it for rice. The people from the cities would go out to the country farmers, take off their coats and leave them, and go home with a sack of potatoes or rice or whatever the farmers had to trade for the coats. We were fortunate that we had a food store and did not starve. We were even able to help people by trading with them.

Six months after I came to Tokyo, I met Auntie's niece and we became friends. She was close to my age and she did not live too far away. In the evenings, after our work was done, I would often go to her house to visit her. We spent many evenings together.

One day, in the Tokyo sky I saw an airplane circling around way up high in the air. It was so small I could hardly see it. I don't know how long it had been in the sky. A neighbor told us he thought it was a B-29 warplane. There was no air raid warning and it did not drop any bombs. We guessed they were taking pictures of the land below.

In a short time the plane disappeared from the sky. I thought it was not safe to live in Tokyo anymore, but I really liked living there by then. Even though I had to work hard, it was fun to be with Auntie now that I had a friend my age.

That night I dreamed that many airplanes came and they dropped bombs on our town. I was trying to run away but my body was frozen and I couldn't move. I hoped it would never happen—such a thing like dropping bombs.

A few months later, air raid sirens started and the radio said there were many B-29 warplanes in the Tokyo area. They came in early morning, late at night, anytime. Mt. Fuji was like a landmark for the planes to turn around and circle back to Tokyo.

Every family made a small bomb shelter by digging into hills or making pits in the ground or under the house. We were in fear of our lives every day. When the radio said the planes were near us, people ran to their shelters and crawled inside. The bomb shelters were dark and damp, not a pleasant place to be.

Auntie's shelter had dirt walls and a dirt floor. The ceiling was made of planks of wood nailed together and was so low we had to crouch down. A wooden frame and door was set into the entrance so the shelter could be shut off from the outside. The tunnel leading down into the shelter was L-shaped to help protect us better from a bomb blast. We kept flashlights and candles in the shelter so we could see in the darkness inside.

One day we were in the shelter and I tried to get back to the house to get important papers from my school days. You could not keep anything in the shelter because it was damp. Suddenly a bomb dropped nearby. The sound was so loud and the earth and the whole house shook like from an earthquake. I fell to the ground, frozen, and saw the windows were shattered. My bad dream had come true! I saw lots of smoke, and the city hall nearby was on fire. The fire got bigger and bigger because most houses were made of wood and burned easily. Soon there were red flames everywhere. Hot ashes came down all over, even on my head. Auntie and I ran and jumped into a nearby river and hid under a concrete bridge until the fire passed us.

The river water was not very deep, but it was dirty with waste water and sewage. It smelled very bad. It was horrible, but we were afraid for our lives and stayed in the river hiding until our skin became wrinkled. I guess you can do anything to survive. Afterwards we went to a friend's house that was not damaged and took cool baths to clean our bodies and then wore borrowed clothes.

My aunt's house and shop were burned down. Everything we had was ruined. Before the bombing, my aunt had gotten a silk kimono for me from the black market as a present because I worked so hard and was a big help to her. I had worn it on New

Year's Day and went to the shrine nearby to pray for our good health and that the war would stop soon and give us peace. I never before had a pretty silk kimono that was new and I was so happy, but after the bomb and big fire I lost all my school report cards, my grade school graduation diploma, my classmates' pictures, my clothes, my new kimono, my diary—everything was gone.

I had to go back to my own house then. The trains were still working. I was so glad to come back home to see my parents and see that they were safe, but I needed a job connected with the government or helping with the war effort because my mother was still so afraid they might draft girls. I heard that a small factory nearby needed helpers for making parts for airplane engines, so I went there and got a job. It was men's work, but there were no young men so mostly young girls worked there.

We worked in an assembly line cutting pipes into small pieces. Then we used machines to make threaded ends on them so they could be connected to other pieces. After enough parts were finished and cleaned, they were loaded into crates. There were a few older men that worked there and they did the heavy-lifting work. The crates were put on three-wheeled iron carts, pushed out to the country-side, and dumped in shallow pits. The pits were covered with straw and then with soil to hide them from enemy planes.

Sometimes when warplanes came to our area we had to stay in the bomb shelter for a long time. The factory shelter was long and narrow. Wooden steps went down to it. It was deep underground and big enough for all the workers. Thin wooden panels were put along the walls and the ceiling was made of wood, but the floor was still dirt. It was pretty nice for a bomb shelter and even had an electric light inside—but no bathroom area. The shelter was under a very large fish pond that had a beautiful landscape around it. We thought if a bomb fell in the pond we would all be drowned.

If we had to stay in the shelter a long time, we had to make up for our time by working later, sometimes to midnight. In the winter, the owner's wife made noodle soup for us. We were so cold and hungry, and the soup tasted so good and made our bodies feel warm.

We were young and had little fear. In the bomb shelter we would sing and some girls would dance. One day, as usual, we ran to the bomb shelter. One of the girls ran back out to the lunchroom to use the bathroom there. We begged her not to go, but she said she had to. All of a sudden a warplane came down from the sky like a hawk to catch a rabbit. It made a terrible loud noise and shot her with its machine gun. She lay quiet and bleeding on the ground and we all screamed and started crying. We ran to help her, but there was nothing we could do. She died at the hospital. She was just a young girl—

why did they shoot her?! After that we were very scared. No one sang songs in the shelter anymore; we just sat still and listened for airplanes.

The Tokorozawa airport was near our town. It was a very small airport with only one short runway that was used for the very first airplanes in Japan. Today it is part of an air museum. I remember that biplanes used to fly from the runway, but during the war the military used the airport. My father and other men from our town had to hide the runway from the enemy airplanes. The men would put pieces of sod on the runway to try to camouflage it. It was a dangerous job because there was nowhere for the men to hide in the open field.

My father said that a man he worked with at the airport was killed by one of the small bombs that a warplane dropped. He was almost killed once, too, but he thought that the gods did take care of him. I begged him, "Please don't do this job," but he said he had to. He was ordered to do the job and he had no choice.

At night my father took turns with other men in town to watch the night sky. The men would listen to the radio and listen for airplanes and use a megaphone to warn the town people of danger. I told my father I hated war and I hated the American military killing innocent civilian mothers and children. We did not ask for war. My father said to me, "Don't hate anyone, it doesn't do any good. They are only doing their duty. This is war." How could he say that?! But I guess we were their enemies and they must try to hurt us.

My parents didn't talk about the war. I don't think they knew much about it except that our leaders thought war was necessary. People were expected to do what they were told and were not to disagree with leaders. We had to respect them.

We believed that Emperor Hirohito was a living god, but he was mostly hidden from us. One day, though, before the war started, he came through our town riding on a white horse and everyone bowed down so low and did not look at his face. We showed him great respect.

Even though the emperor was our ruler, the military leaders seemed to make all the decisions and we had to obey. Prime Minister Hideki Tojo was a very powerful man in charge of the military. We could not speak against Japan or the leaders. That would be a dangerous thing to do because you could be arrested or even killed.

Civilians had to learn how to protect themselves. We were taught to relay buckets of water to stop fires. We had to practice that often because if a bomb was dropped there was so much danger of fire spreading through the wooden buildings of the town. Also, we had long bamboo poles with sharp points and we were taught to use them as weapons when the Americans came. But, it would be impossible to defend ourselves from the soldiers' guns with bamboo poles!

Our country did not have much gasoline anymore so many buses in our area began to use wood to run the engines. A compartment for burning wood was built onto the front side of the bus, on the opposite side from the driver. A pipe came out of the top of the compartment to let out the smoke.

Each bus had a busgirl that would take tickets and money and announce the stops. She would also get off at the stops to load more wood into the fuel compartment. The bus carried wood on a shelf underneath it.

My cousin was a busgirl before the war and I thought that would be a fun job. The girls had a uniform to wear of a navy blue skirt and white blouse. I thought I would like to punch tickets and wear a pretty uniform someday.

Lots of times from late morning to late afternoon the town would turn off the electricity to save energy. At night we mostly used kerosene lamps or candles. Even now candlelight is not romantic to me; it brings up wartime memories. For many years after, I would hear in my head the sound of warplanes coming whenever I saw candlelight.

At night when warning sirens started, we would turn off our lights or cover any electric lights with dark material to help hide the brightness from outside the windows. We thought the town would be hidden. I don't think it mattered because the B-29's would drop parachutes that carried bright flares to light up a whole town, and then drop bombs.

Sometimes we stayed a long time in the bomb shelter until the airplanes went away from our area. Sometimes we skipped our meal because there was no time to cook lunch or dinner. If our meal was interrupted, my mother would say, "Eat first, eat first!" She did not want us to waste food, but I could not eat when the sirens were going. My father would say, "Oh-oh, we have guests!"

I was scared a lot. We could not have a good night's sleep. We had no peace of mind. Who wanted war anyway?

One winter night, the town of Hachioji, not too far from us, was bombed and it seemed like the whole town was burning. The sky was glowing red and was filled with clouds of smoke. My father and I stood outside on a little hill and watched from the distance. My teeth were chattering with fear and cold. That night I couldn't sleep at all. I felt so sad for the people who died. I imagined children and babies covered with flames and dying. I was so frightened that the next day I was still upset and could not eat breakfast.

One day my girlfriend and I decided to get permanents for our hair. I was excited. We had pigtails all the time and only wore dark simple clothes to help hide us from the enemy airplanes, but we were young girls and we wanted to look nice for a change. My mother warned me, "How silly to go get your hair done. It is dangerous to go out in the fields. You can't hear the radio warnings."

We went anyway. We took a paper bag with a little charcoal for the hairdresser to burn to make heat to do the permanents because the utility company turned off electricity in the daytime. We rode our bicycles down the road between farmers' fields. On one side there were soybeans; on the other side there were tea bushes.

On the way, we heard airplane noise so we rode faster down the gravel road. The noise got louder and louder and we rode faster and faster until the sound was so close that we jumped from our bikes and tried to hide under the tea bushes. One plane flew down low and shot at our bikes and made flat tires. We were very lucky we did not get killed.

We had to push our bikes down the road to the hairdresser's house. It was supposed to take a half hour to get there but we took twice as long. Then we had to push our bikes back home. We were so exhausted. My mother said, "See, I told you so. You girls are crazy. Your life is more important than curly hair!"

The war was finally over in August, 1945, after the atomic bombs were dropped on Hiroshima and Nagasaki. The radio announced only that the cities were hit by a new type of bomb the Americans had and the damage was very bad. That's all I knew. I did not know much else about that until many, many years later when I visited the Nagasaki Atomic Bomb Museum. The things I learned there and the pictures I saw made me feel sick. I hoped that no one would ever use an atomic bomb again.

At noon time on August 15, Emperor Hirohito spoke to the people. For the first time in history a Japanese emperor spoke to his people! He spoke in an old-style formal way, not like the everyday language, and the message was a tape recording. I did not hear him speaking, but I know that many people in our town could not understand him very well because of the bad recording and the strange way of speaking. He announced on the radio that the war was over—not whether we won or lost, just that the war was over and an agreement was made.

I was so happy! Most people in our town were excited and relieved. They cheered and hugged each other. Many people were just glad the war was over. We were all tired of war.

After the War

After the war, my mother asked my brother and me to see if her sister was still alive. She lived in the town of Ueno, which is a part of Tokyo. Our town was very lucky it did not have much damage, but we heard that a lot of Tokyo was destroyed by bombs and fire and that much of the city was in ashes.

My mother made rice balls wrapped in dried seaweed for our box lunches. We took the train to the Ueno Park station. We were going to eat lunch in the park there and then look for our aunt.

The area was damaged very badly. Many buildings were crumbled or knocked down. We got to the park and sat on a bench and started to eat. I wrinkled my nose and I told my brother, "It smells here, something terrible." Then we saw a beggar dragging himself on the ground towards us, so weak, nothing but bones. He couldn't even talk. He opened his hands, asking for food. We were so scared by the sight that we jumped up and threw our food on the ground and ran away with our hearts pounding. But, as we ran we saw in a corner of the park there were big piles of dead people—men and women, young and old, even children—some black from fire and others in tattered clothes. It was horrible to see!

We found where my aunt's house was, but it was destroyed. We hoped that she was not dead. Later my aunt wrote a letter to my mother to say she was okay. She was staying at a shelter with many other people.

Sometimes I think about the poor beggar man and I wonder if he survived. We were too scared to think about helping him. The memory of the park is one I wish I could forget. It is like a nightmare that is hiding in my head. War is such a terrible thing.

In September, our town saw American Military Police walking around on the streets. We had never seen American people before. They were so tall and had such long legs! Some men had skin so white and some men had skin so dark.

As the days went by, more and more soldiers came into the town, just walking around. We were afraid of them. They all carried big long guns. When I saw them I ran into the house and closed the door and hid until they went away.

The Americans occupied the Irumagawa military base near our town. They named it Johnson Air Base for a colonel who was a military hero but he died in a plane crash right after the war. There were a lot of military areas around us during the war and the

Americans took them over. Toyooka Airfield at Irumagawa had a school for training young pilots, especially kamikaze pilots later in the war. That was a very sad thing, to have the young men learn to fly to their deaths. Many of those men were college students. I guess Japan was getting desperate to win the war. The men had no choice; if they refused they would dishonor their families and their country. It was considered a great honor and a duty to die for Japan. That is what we were told by our leaders.

The more I saw the American soldiers, the less I was afraid. We got used to seeing them. The soldiers were kind to the children; sometimes they would pass out sticks of chewing gum or pieces of chocolate. That was a big treat!

On the weekends, though, some of the soldiers would do mischief. One night a drunken soldier came into our back yard and peed in our water well. My mother was very upset and the next day she called the town office. Men came to put some kind of disinfectant in the well. We couldn't use our well for a week.

Once a young American man came to my father's shop and wanted to sell him some American cigarettes. My father bought a package. My mother said to him, "Now, you know better. You are not to buy anything from them." He said, "Oh, you know that young man may need some money. He is far away from home." My father did not smoke, but he thought maybe he could give the cigarettes to his customers.

Six months after the war was over, I found a job as a waitress in the American Officers' Club at Johnson Air Base. One hundred people applied for fifteen jobs available, and I was selected. I was very lucky.

I was excited, but when I went home and told my mother, she said, "You don't work in those places. It is dangerous for young girls to work where all those soldiers are." I told her, "I promise I will be safe. I need a job." The job paid five dollars a month. That was a lot of money back then.

Before we could work as waitresses, we had to have physical examinations. We were also taught just enough English for our job services. We would carry a little piece of paper in our pockets that had basic English we could use to talk to the Americans. "Would you like some more coffee?" "Are you finished, Sir?" There was an interpreter there from Hawaii who would help us with our speaking.

One time an American man winked at one of the waitresses and she wondered what the signal meant. The interpreter laughed and said that meant the man was being charming to her. We did think the Americans had such big eyes and long charming eyelashes.

The woman in charge of the waitresses found out that I could sew. Material was expensive then so she gave me American parachutes to cut up to make fifteen uniforms. The blouses were made from white material, and the skirts were made from bright blue material. They were very pretty.

I worked in the day and came home in late afternoon. There was a good system for girls to feel safe going back and forth to work. When we got off at the train station near to the air base, there would be a military truck waiting to take us to the Officer's Club. When we left work, a truck took us back to the train station. All of us young girls would sing in the truck. I really liked this job. I made some good friends and I learned some English.

Sometimes the kitchen crew would give the girls leftover food to take home. My mother would not eat any of it, but my father thought the American food tasted good. He had never had any before. He told me to tell Cook, "I thank you for the good food my daughter brought to me. We haven't had good food for a long time. That was a special treat."

The waitresses ate lunch at the Officers' Club so I didn't have to take a box lunch. I had never eaten chicken with bones in it before. I felt like a savage. It took me a long time to get used to it. I always removed the meat from the bones before eating it. Most of the food was good.

One day while serving tables at the Officer's Club I met a Catholic priest. He was an old man. I was impressed that he spoke Japanese. I asked him, "Where did you learn Japanese? You speak very well." He said, "I was living at a Japanese farm house during the war. I could not get back to America so I stayed at the farm house as part of the family. I wore Japanese clothes and learned the language. The family helped to keep me safe." He started telling me about the Christian religion. I was interested in what he was saying to me. He never did come back again, though.

For a while, after I left work I would take a forty-five-minute train ride to take a clothing design class from a dressmaker. I would come home on the last train of the night, very hungry and tired. My mother would save food for me, but it was cold. It would be hard for me to get up the next morning.

After that class was over, I did not take any more classes because it was too hard for me to work and go to school. I had learned all that I really wanted to know anyway. The class taught me how to create and design my own clothes. I became a very good seamstress and I could make my own patterns and sew whatever I wanted to.

One day at work, the interpreter asked me if I knew someone who could make little girls' dresses. I said, "Yes, I like sewing." She said, "Captain Bauer is looking for someone who can sew for his little daughter."

The daughter had a deformed arm and could not wear already-made clothes from the store. The captain said he would pay me ten dollars a month. That was twice what I was making as a waitress! His family had not come to Japan yet, but as soon as they came he would like for me to work for them. I would have to live at their house or at a dormitory because he lived at a different air base farther away. I promised to work for him later, when he needed me.

My father was so kind to me. I had to get up at six o-clock in the morning to get ready for work. In the winter when I went outside to wash my face in the cold well water, my father warmed up a towel for me to dry off with. He would put my shoes in the sunshine to get them warm before I put them on. One day I forgot to take the napkin that I wore over my arm at work. He came on a bicycle to the train station and he said, "You forgot the napkin. I am sure you need it." I said to him, "Thank you, Father." I did not tell him that I had a spare one at work.

When I was about twenty-two years old, my father became ill. My mother took him to the doctor. There was not a bus or train to the doctor's office so they had to walk.

The first time they went there, the doctor said maybe my father did not have enough nutrition. He gave him a certain kind of vitamin, but my father did not get better. He got worse, so my mother took him to the doctor again. They didn't come home for a long time. I told my brother, "Go ride the bike and check to see where they are."

When my brother came back home, he told me our father was dizzy and could not walk. He was sitting with our mother on a bench at the temple garden, resting until he had enough breath to walk. They finally came home. After that my father could not get up anymore.

My mother contacted another doctor. We did not have a telephone so she went to a neighbor's house to use theirs. The doctor came to our house and checked my father. He said there was nothing he could do for him. He told us to put my father's feet up higher than his head. "If his face gets red and he snores, that means the blood is not going to the brain."

Soon my father could not talk anymore. His body would not move well. I brought him food from the Officers' Club. My mother mashed it and spooned it into his mouth. He loved the fruit cocktail. He could not talk to me, but he would show me a half-smile expression.

Very early one morning, several weeks after he became ill, my father made a funny noise and stopped snoring. My mother always checked his every movement, but no one could help him now. At my father's funeral, there were so many people because my father was kind to everyone. My mother didn't know half the people there.

It was May, when the peony flowers bloom, and so there were many big peony blossoms of soft pink and white to decorate the funeral. They smelled so sweet. The peony flower blooms for a short while and then all the petals fall at once, like a life that suddenly is cut short.

My father was fifty-nine years old when he died. I felt the whole world was dark; he was the sunshine to me. It was very hard to overcome his death. Even now, sometimes I look at his picture and I talk to him and cry. I feel very sad that I did not ever tell my father that I loved him. In Japan, we did not hug or kiss; we bowed, even to our parents.

Someday I wanted to marry a man who was the image of my father who was so good, always giving kindness. I will always remember my father's love. I keep it in my heart.

Captain Bauer finally came to the Officers' Club to tell me that his wife wanted to see me. He brought his wife and introduced me to her and their baby daughter. The little girl's name was Barbara and she was about eighteen months old. She was a very cute blonde-haired girl. She was born with an extra bone in her left arm and seven fingers and no thumb on that hand. She had to wear a cast on her wrist. The parents wished that some day when she was older she could have surgery to make her arm and hand more normal.

I quit the waitress job and moved in with the Captain's family. They lived near Tachikawa Air Base. It was farther away from my home than the Johnson Base. I made baby clothes almost full-time, but the wife, Ann, also taught me to cook American food, and so I cooked some for the family and was paid even more.

The family was from the American South so I learned how to cook turnip greens with bacon fat, black-eyed peas, cornbread and biscuits. They loved beans and ham hocks. I hated that, but I had to eat it because I ate supper with the family.

I met a friend, Junko, who worked for the family next door. She took the train back and forth from her home outside Tokyo. Sometimes we would trade lunches—she liked beans. I only would see her at lunch, but we became good friends. I kept in touch with her for many years.

A lot of Japanese people worked at the American air bases and hospitals and many of the married American servicemen had "houseboys" to work for their families and women to work as maids or baby-sitters. Everyone seemed to get along okay together. It was hard to believe that we were once enemies.

Sometimes my friends and I would go to the army base for dances there. Trucks would come to the train station to pick up Japanese girls for the soldiers to dance with and then take them back to the station later. I went to some of the dances just to have fun watching because I couldn't dance in the American style.

At one dance I met an American soldier there from Indiana. He asked me to come some evenings to the ballpark nearby and sit on a bench with him and then he would teach me some American religion. He taught me about the Bible. He found a Bible for us to study that was written in both Japanese and English.

One day the soldier invited me to go to the small chapel at the air base for a Sunday morning church service. After that, he took me often. He was a nice gentleman.

The more I went to the chapel, the more I liked the American religion. My friend told me, "Strong faith can move rocks, so be strong. I am going back to America pretty soon. I hope you remember all I said to you."

When it was time for my friend to go home, he came to see me and gave me the Bible that was written in English and Japanese. He also gave me a little pocket-size book of inspiration. He said to me, "Trust in God."

I told my mother that I had met an American soldier who told me all about the American religion. I said, "I think I'm going to believe the American religion instead of the Japanese religion." Before that, I didn't really believe in any religion. My mother said, "It doesn't matter what your religious belief, as long as you are facing your god. That's more important than my religion or your religion." So I began to believe more the way I thought Americans believed.

I worked for Captain Bauer for about two-and-a-half years, and then his wife had to go back to the United States. I missed the baby very much. Several years later they came back to see me. The wife came all the way to my hometown to show me their daughter. In California, the little girl had an operation so that the arm and hand looked much more normal. She did not remember me.

I worked many years for different American officers' families. Mostly I lived in their homes during the week doing cooking and sewing. Once I lived in one of the dormitories set up by the air bases for workers to live in. There were many young girls staying there and it was very noisy. I was more used to quiet so I did not stay there very long.

For a little while I worked for a Chinese-American lieutenant. His wife was Chinese and very tiny so I sewed all her clothes, and in a Chinese style. She would go to the city of Yokohama to the Chinese section to play Mahjong, an old Chinese game. She would take me with her so she would have someone to travel with. She played Mahjong until very very late in the night and then slept late in the morning. I would walk along the streets to see the city a little.

Most of the time, the families recommended me to their friends when it was time for them to go back to America. The families were very kind and nice and I enjoyed working for them. They helped me to learn more English. Lots of times they gave me gifts for my birthday and Christmas. Before going back to America they would give me a nice gift to thank me for all the help. I kept all the gifts in my dresser at home.

One day I went to visit my sister and before I went home she said to me, "Do you check in your dresser once in awhile just to be sure everything is safe?" I thought that was a strange thing to say, but I went home and I looked in my dresser.

I was surprised to see a gold watch and a sweater missing from my drawers, also some of the money I was saving. I asked my mother who stole my money and the nice sweater that was a Christmas gift. My mother said, "Oh, you must have lost them." Then I accused my mother and finally she told me my brother took them from me and gave them to his girlfriend. I was very upset.

After that, I could not trust my family. No matter right or wrong, my mother would stick with my brother because he was the son and she loved him more than me. The son is supposed to take care of the parents so she wanted to be nice to him.

I did not go out and rent a room because I would only be there on the weekends. My brother kept stealing from me. I complained to him and he yelled at me and told me to leave. The house belonged to my mother, but my brother acted like the house was his.

My brother did not work for several years because he was disabled by a truck accident and also he had an ulcer. He also had very bad eyesight—I think that is why he was not drafted in the war. He used my money to buy things for himself. I was giving my mother half of my paycheck anyway, so I did not have much money for myself after my brother would take some too.

I was very upset about my brother's behavior and I wanted to get away from home. I wanted to get married and leave home, but I did not get out much to meet people. Also, there weren't many men my age left after the war.

One day, a friend asked me to go with her to dance lessons at Johnson Air Base. At one of the lessons, an American man named Allen came to ask me to dance. I said, "I can't dance." He said, "I can't either. We can learn together."

We were partners for a month or two every Wednesday evening, and then he asked me to go out for a Saturday afternoon. He introduced me to his roommate, Bob, and we all went for a rowboat ride on a nearby river.

It was funny, but I had met Bob before at a dance. Some soldiers were teasing me because I could not dance—so why was I at a dance? I felt shy and embarrassed. Bob saved me from them and asked me to teach him some Japanese. He taught me some English words. I didn't see him again until the boat ride. After that, the three of us went out almost every Saturday afternoon.

Allen was leaving for the United States in eight more months, so he only wanted to be a friend and for me to translate Japanese for him. He and Bob were nice people and it was fun to be with them. They loved Japan and wanted to see all they could.

The three of us went to Tokyo Park and the Museum of Natural History and other places. By then the area had mostly been built back up from the war damage. I had a nice time with them. I had never been many places in Tokyo so it was a special treat for me. We had lunch at restaurants sometimes. They loved Japanese food. I was surprised to see how well they used chopsticks.

One Saturday, Bob did not come with Allen. I dated Allen until he went back to the United States. He went to the University of Michigan. After he left, he wrote a letter to me once a week. Sometimes I had to ask a friend how to spell English words so I could write back to him. Every time I wrote a letter, I added, "P.S. Can you understand my writing?" On Valentine's Day Allen sent me a beautiful card and a gold necklace that had a heart pendant with a tiny pearl in the center. It was very pretty.

Allen wrote to me for about a year. Then one day he wrote to me to come to the United States so we could get married there. I was scared to go to America by myself so he said that he would come to Japan to marry me.

I always wanted to marry a man like my father and wished some day I could meet someone like him—kind heart, sincere, patient. But there was no Japanese man for me. So many men my age died in the war. Thanks to God, I found Allen.

A New Life

I was happy, but my mother was not. She was ashamed that her daughter was dating an American man, and when Allen came for me she would not let him in her house. She said to me, "American men do not take responsibility. The men take Japanese girls to America and then dump them. You will see. That's what I heard. You will live far away so if something happens to you, who will help you?"

I told my mother, "I don't believe he would do such a thing. He is like my father. He is kind-of-heart, an honest man. The only difference is that he is American." I was very upset about my mother.

The rest of my family was also not happy that I was going to marry an American man. My middle sister's husband said to me, "Are you going to marry my enemy? You know I lost my brother in the war."

Only my oldest sister's family said they wished me happiness. Ine said, "Sometimes even marriage to a Japanese man does not work out as well as we want. If things don't work out with your marriage, you are welcome to come back to our house. Our door will be open for you." I started to cry.

In May, 1958, Allen and I went to the American Embassy in Tokyo to get married. I did not expect my family to give us a party or congratulate us. I felt very sad. Allen and I rented a small house and our landlord gave us a little party. My oldest sister gave us money as a wedding gift. The American family I was working for gave us a farewell wedding gift of a beautiful blanket and sheets.

We stayed in the little rented house for a short while and lived in the Japanese way. I asked my mother to please make my husband a yukata, the informal cotton kimono. She did even though she did not like that I married him. The kimono was dark blue and hand-stitched. Allen liked to take a bath in the evening and relax afterwards wearing the kimono. He liked to try to follow the Japanese customs.

We had a very long honeymoon from mid-June to mid-September. Allen planned the best places to go. He knew Japan better than I did! We went to the resort area of Toi, on the western side of the Izu peninsula, and stayed at a hotel with beautiful rooms. Allen would put on a blue and white yukata that was from the hotel. He would wear geta shoes to walk around the outside areas of the hotel.

The maid would bring breakfast and dinner to the room. One evening we went to the dining room. There was so much to eat! The waitresses kept bringing us more and more food. The room and all the good service we had was three dollars a day. The view from the hotel was very beautiful, overlooking the ocean.

One day we went out on a boat with some fishermen that were catching squid. They did not catch very many so they gave them to us. The hotel chef cooked some of them for part of our dinner, but some he left raw for us to try— we did not like that!

We went sightseeing all around the Izu peninsula. We took the trains to Atami and Shuzenji and we relaxed in outdoor pools there that were warmed by hot springs. We also went to the Hakone mountain area and the Kawaguchi Lake resort close to Mt. Fuji. They were such peaceful places with beautiful views. It was a special treat for me to see all these beautiful places because I had never been on a vacation. Even though I had grown up in Japan, I had never really been outside my home town area except for the trips to Tokyo with Allen.

Once in awhile, we stopped at the house we had rented or at my oldest sister's house to wash our dirty clothes. Then we repacked our suitcases and we took off traveling again. We had a wonderful time for three months.

I was a little worried about what the Japanese people would think about Allen and me, but people were very friendly to us. Children would smile and sometimes say, "Hello"—it was the only American word they knew. Allen knew some Japanese words and some short sentences. He had an English-Japanese dictionary that he carried with him. He was not afraid to travel anywhere in Japan. At that time there were a lot of signs in English because of the Occupation.

The day before leaving Japan, we went to the cemetery to see my father's grave. I knelt down and told my father, "My dear Father, I married an American man. I know you are surprised to hear about it. After you were gone from me I missed you so much, and someday I wanted to marry a man the image of you. I love him and I'm sure he loves me. Please forgive me." Then I cried, and Allen was behind me with tears in his eyes.

On September fifteenth, we left from Yokohama Harbor to go to the United States across the Pacific Ocean. Our big ship was named "President Wilson." It took two weeks to get there. I thought I would have fun riding a big ship, but the first three or four days I was seasick and could not enjoy the trip at all.

On the fourth day, I felt a little better and went on the deck and met a young French man. He was very friendly. I chatted with him a little in English. He was a newspaper journalist and traveled to many countries. He said, "I would like to settle down some day. If I marry, I would like to marry a Japanese girl." I asked why he wanted a Japanese girl. He said, "Because the Japanese ladies are very graceful and I love their customs." He gave me his business card.

After I began to feel better from the seasickness, I sure did enjoy the trip. Most of the people were very friendly. Every night there was a show or movie There was music and dancing, too. We would sit on the deck during the day and talk with new friends we made. On Sunday there was a church service. Day after day we saw blue ocean and blue sky. We never did see a whale, but we did see flying fish jumping out of the water.

One evening my husband and I stayed on the deck for awhile. A full moon was reflecting on the ocean, calm and peaceful. I saw the propeller at the end of the ship stirring up a mysterious white light glowing in the water. It was the strangest light I had ever seen and I could not think what it was. I asked my husband about it and he said maybe it was the propeller stirring up small jellyfish that made the light. I wished the moment would last forever.

Then one day we saw the Hawaiian Islands. The ship stopped just for a short while so we did not have time to sightsee. We got off the ship and I had a hot dog, French fries and root beer for lunch. I had American fast food for the first time. It was good. I told my husband, "I wish I could eat hot dogs everyday!" He thought that was funny.

The big ship finally arrived in San Francisco. We went right to the Greyhound station to take a bus to Chicago. It was a very long ride. America was a very big country! On the way, my husband decided to stop by to visit his old army friend in Minnesota. He lived on a farm with his mother. They gave us a warm welcome and showed us around the farm. It was big. They showed me how to milk a cow. They took us to their church and invited us to a church dinner. They were such nice people, I could not help loving them.

The friend's mother took us to her oldest son's house and introduced his family. I asked her, "If your son told you he was going to marry a Japanese girl, what would you think about that? Would you be happy?" She said, "Oh, dear child, you are so sweet. I don't think you have anything to worry about. If you are not accepted in the family, come to stay with us. I would love to have you." I only knew her for such a short time, but I felt so comfortable with her. The mother's kindness touched my heart, and I will always remember her.

We finally arrived in the big city of Chicago. We took a small bus to Allen's parents' house in the Chicago suburb of River Grove. His brother came to meet us at the bus stop. When I met the parents, I felt afraid and bashful—especially with my new mother-in-law.

I guess I was worrying for nothing, because after a few days I felt comfortable. I thought my mother-in-law liked me all right. My father-in-law liked me, too. He was a very quiet man who would hardly ever talk, but he would show me a smile and pat my head. Allen's cousin, Theresa, lived nearby and was very warm and friendly to me. She would say, "Oh, look how well she speaks English!" and other nice things to try to help me fit in with the family. I liked her a lot.

Even though I had lived with American families, I still had much to learn about America. Some of the food I was not used to. For breakfast we had cereal and orange juice. "Orange juice will freshen your mouth," my mother-in-law would say. I learned to like it. I did not like cold cereal, though, and I thought that oatmeal was horrible, but I had to be polite and eat it.

I did not like the American rice, either. One day my husband went to Chicago and bought a bag of short-grain Japanese rice for me. I cooked some for the family and they loved it. My mother-in-law would tell her friends what good rice I cooked—so fluffy! I would also cook some stir-fry dinners that I learned to make from the Chinese woman I worked for near Johnson Air Base.

In Japan, we do not say the word "no" very much because that would not be polite. We say, "yes, please," or "yes, I don't want anymore." When the American people asked me a question I would not always understand the way they said it and I would say, "yes," even though I meant "no." That would get me into trouble sometimes.

My mother-in-law was waiting to give me a bridal shower, but she never did tell me about it. One night her sister-in-law called me and asked if I could come over to her house to show her an easy way to do a crochet stitch. But that evening I had washed my hair and I had curlers all over my head. My husband said it would not take too long; his aunt just wanted to know how to start a simple stitch.

We went to the aunt's house. When we got there, it was so quiet and no one was in the front room. My husband said maybe she was in the basement. I went downstairs. There was a small watering can hanging from the ceiling above a paper umbrella that had pretty streamers coming down from it like rain. Lots of people were there and they shouted, "Surprise!"

Oh, I wish I had known before I came to her house, but no one told me it was a bridal shower. They had to explain to me what it was because Japan did not have such a tradition. Everyone was dressed so nice, and I was with no makeup and had curlers on my head. I wished my husband had given me a little hint!

There were so many beautiful gifts. I appreciated so much all the American people being so kind to me. Now all we needed was a house. We lived with my in-laws until my husband could get a job and we could save some money. They fixed up their basement for us to live in. I didn't always like living so close to my in-laws and trying to be quiet and not bother them, but it was a good way to save up money. I met many people who were friendly and kind, and my mother-in-law helped me get to know

American customs. One day I asked her what she thought about her son marrying a Japanese girl. She said that at first she was not too happy, but it was her son's decision and she would accept it. And so she was a nice mother-in-law to me.

My mother-in-law's parents came from Holland to the United States. She had two brothers who lived nearby. My father-in-law was born in Holland and his family moved to America when he was a teenager. He had a brother and two sisters that would visit. They all lived where there were a lot of other Dutch people.

Relatives and friends and neighbors would stop by often for coffee and visiting. They liked me and would touch my hair and talk about how thick and shiny it was. They would say, "Oh, look how cute she is!" It was a little strange for me and sometimes I felt like a pet, but they were nice people.

My mother-in-law belonged to a Dutch Christian Reformed church with a very strict religion. You could do nothing on Sunday—not go to a movie, cut the grass, or sew. My husband and I did not follow such a strict religion, and his father did not go to church at all. This bothered my mother-in-law, but she did not say too much about it. We did have to follow her rules and rest on Sundays, though. We prayed at every meal and read from the Bible after dinner each night.

In July, 1959, I had a baby girl in a hospital on the lakefront of downtown Chicago. When my husband came to see me the night the baby was born, he brought a dozen yellow roses to me and a box of candy to the nurses.

I named the baby "Linda." When she was first born she looked at me with big dark eyes as if to say, "Who are you?" I forgot all about the difficult birth. I loved her very much and I loved being a mother.

The relatives and visitors all loved the baby. I would sew pretty dresses for her to wear. She always looked beautiful. I would push her in a stroller down the sidewalk and people would stop us. They would smile at the baby and ask me, "Where did you come from?" It was such a nice neighborhood and the people were so friendly.

When I first came to America I was afraid of being in a strange and different country. I was afraid of how the people would look at me because I looked so different from them and because my country was once their enemy. The American people I met in Japan during the Occupation were nice so I hoped that the people in the United States would be nice also, and they were. It was not until I was an old woman that I met someone that said to me, "You are Japanese? I hate Japanese! My brother was killed in the war." I was hurt, and I told the older woman, "I had nothing to do with the war. I did not want war. Everyone is hurt in war." Most people accepted me, though. Maybe it helped that I came to America thirteen years after the war was over; people had time to forgive and understand that no one likes war.

In a year or so, we had a house built for us in a different town. Even before the house was finished, I designed a garden with a patio and a small fishpond with a little waterfall. Now this is a popular thing in America, but at the time it was unusual.

The patio became a beautiful place to relax. On summer evenings, sitting on the bench watching the pretty goldfish and listening to the water trickle down the rocks gave us such a peaceful feeling. In winter, red cardinals were a pretty contrast to white snow that covered the patio and the evergreens.

My husband built a Japanese "tokonoma" art area inside the house. This is a very important decoration area in Japanese guest rooms. We put it in the living room. We put on the wall a long silk scroll with a landscape painting that was a present from my sister. On a shelf below it, I always kept a simple Japanese-style "ikebana" flower arrangement. We couldn't make the tokonoma as beautiful as the Japanese style, but we did the best we could.

In March, 1961, not too long after we moved into our new house, we had another baby girl. We named her "Kathleen," but we called her "Kathy," and she was a very happy baby who laughed a lot.

My girls were only twenty-one months apart and I liked to sew dresses for them that were the same so that they looked almost like twins. When they started going to school, sometimes their teachers took them to the principal to show her their dresses.

My daughters did not learn to speak Japanese. I wanted to speak only English because America was my new country. I wanted to take English lessons, but my husband liked the way I talked and thought it wasn't necessary for me to learn perfect English. I did teach the girls how to count to ten in Japanese and to say some basic words, like "konnichi wa," which is "good day," and "arigato," which is "thank you." I taught them some Japanese children's folk-songs that I sang when I was a child. I also told them stories of when I was a little girl growing up in Japan, and told them many wise sayings that my mother told me.

The children thought the Japanese language was very hard to learn. Also, there were not many people in the area that looked foreign, so the girls wanted to fit in with their friends and not be different. That was a little hard to do in the summer when they turned so brown in the sun.

The girls did not have much problem fitting in, though. They were shy, but they had friends. One day I came to their school to speak to all the children about Japan. My girls were embarrassed about that.

Sometimes my husband would drive me to Chicago to the Japanese section of the city, around North Clark Street and Old Town. I loved the restaurants and gift stores there. The children would beg to please eat McDonald's hamburgers instead of the Kamehachi restaurant food that was a big treat for me, but they liked to look in the gift stores. Their favorite was the Toguri store. It smelled like incense. The girls liked to buy little Japanese toys or rice cracker snacks or the chewy Botan candy that had a small prize in the box, and they would look at the many interesting items of the Japanese culture. I would buy thick Japanese magazines to take home.

I loved the grocery stores very much. I was so happy and excited to buy Japanese food to take home and cook. The Star Market was like an old-style Japanese store with a cement floor and big barrels and boxes and shelves filled with food. The children liked to look at all the strange food packages and the different kinds of fish kept on crushed ice. I felt guilty because the groceries were expensive, but my husband knew I missed my home country's food and would let me buy what I wanted. He enjoyed the Japanese food, too.

On our tenth anniversary, my husband said we should go to Japan to see my family. We left our two girls with Allen's brother's family and we went to Japan. We thought the children would be much happier staying in the United States because they could not understand the Japanese language and they did not like to eat the Japanese food.

My family was so happy to see us and to see that I was happy. My oldest sister's family gave a welcome party for us. My mother was there. Her dream of staying with her son in her home did not come true. My brother married and my mother and her new daughter-in-law did not get along. My brother sided with his wife.

My sisters' families had a meeting and decided that my mother would come to live with my oldest sister. My family did not speak to my brother much anymore because he was like the "black sheep." He did not do his duty well to his mother.

My mother called me into the kitchen and she whispered to me, "I am sorry. All the while I was wrong. I do love you, Yaeko. I just did not know how to show my feelings. I was all wrapped up in my son. Please forgive me...I was wrong." I told her, "Mother, I still love you. My love for you never stopped. You are the only mother I have in the whole world." My mother cried.

I felt better after we expressed our feelings to each other. Six months later she died, but I had no hard feelings for her. I was glad that I had forgiven her for the way she treated me, even though I still felt pain in my heart.

We had such a good time in Japan. Both of my sisters welcomed us. We went to stay with each of their families. My husband loved my little niece, Kyoko. She was a very cute and sweet little girl who was almost the same age as our daughter Linda. We stayed two weeks and did a lot of sightseeing.

Many years later, my family began to speak to my brother again. His wife had died so he went to live with his son's family, but he did not get along with them. He was an unhappy man. My sisters told me that he wanted to see me. I was a Christian and I knew I should forgive him, so the next time I went to visit Japan I talked to him on the telephone. He acted like nothing was wrong and blamed my mother for his bad behavior. I felt that he was still the same old person, and I still did not want to see him after how he had treated me.

• • • • •

I had a very happy life for many years. I stayed at home to take care of the children and the house. Allen would drive me to wherever I needed to go. We went on family vacations to many places.

I began to take night classes at a high school so that I could study American history and the Constitution. I wanted to be a United States citizen. I took the classes with two other friends, one from England and one from Vietnam. Our husbands took turns driving us to the classes. In May, 1969, we all went to the courthouse in Chicago and took our citizenship tests. We all passed! We were so proud and happy.

The next-door neighbors had a party for me. There was a large American flag in their living room and there was a cake decorated like the flag. Red, white and blue colors were everywhere. All our neighbor friends congratulated me. It was a happy celebration.

I enjoyed my life very much. I had a good husband and wonderful children. I enjoyed cooking and sewing and painting and doing crafts. Our neighborhood was a friendly place and neighbors would get together for coffee or parties or playing cards. There were fish-fries when our husbands came back from fishing trips in Michigan.

My mother always said to me, "Be good to your husband. He will bring food for the table." I remembered the words very well. I gave him everything he needed. I was a good cook and a good housekeeper. I saved our money. I even polished my husband's shoes. I washed the car. I cut his hair. Before going to bed, I would pick out his clothes and hang them on the doorknob for the next day. He used to say, "I'm a lucky man. You treat me like a king." He would tell everyone that.

Allen was a good husband and father. He gave me beautiful cards for my birthday and Valentine's Day. When he went out of town for work, he called me every night. He would read books to the children at bedtime and help them with homework. In the winter he would make snow igloos and pull the girls on a sled down the street.

Allen was very proud of his wife and his children. But something went wrong. After many years he became unhappy with his life. One day he left home and never came back to me.

It was 1976, and the children were in high school when Allen left. I was very sad and very afraid. My husband used to take care of me, but now my friends had to teach me how to be on my own. I had to get a job and learn how to pay bills and balance the checkbook. I was glad that I had finally insisted years ago that my husband teach me how to drive—even though the girls were scared and would cry in the back seat while I practiced.

Worst of all, it was hard for me not to know English very well. I tried to take a night class to learn English at a Catholic school. The nuns felt sorry for me and were so kind and caring, but I was too upset to learn anything. Also, I think because I was older and I was used to saying many things the incorrect way, it was more difficult for me to learn the language the right way. It is so hard for me to read and write English—I wish so much that I had learned when I first came to America.

I was embarrassed to tell my sisters that my husband had left me. I felt that I had failed and had shamed my family. In Japan it is a terrible thing to bring dishonor to the family. My sisters were very kind to me, though, when I finally told them the bad news. My middle sister began to cry when I told her.

I loved my husband. He was the whole world to me. When I lost my father, I felt so sad and I will never forget him; there was an empty place in my heart. But when I lost my husband, knowing he rejected my love was the worst kind of loss. For many years I wondered how I could live without him. My heart was broken. It still hurts very much to remember him.

I thank God for saving me. I wanted to die, but God closed one door and he opened another. I became much closer to God. He sent me many good friends who have been very kind to me. They encouraged me, and they helped me live through very bad times. I am fortunate that everywhere I go there are good friends. I call them my earth angels. I love them all and I thank them for all they have done for me.

Both my daughters have grown up to be kind and thoughtful people that I am proud of. They help me and encourage me. They still see their father. They married American men who like Japanese food. Sometimes I miss Japan and my family there, but I'm glad I have two wonderful girls who care about me and gave me grandchildren to love. I have bad memories, but I have many good memories to treasure, and I have to always look forward to the future.

Appendix I

Japanese Children's Songs

Shojoji no Tanuki Bayashi
(Tanuki Dance at Shojoji Temple)

Music by Nakayama Shinpei, Words by Noguchi Ujo

Sho-, Sho-, Shojoji
Shojoji no niwa-wa.
Tsu, tsu, tsuki yo da,
Minna dete koi, koi, koi.
Oira no tomodacha,
Pon pok-a-pon-o, pon, pon.

A tanuki is a wild dog-type animal that resembles a raccoon or badger. Here, the tanuki sings:

"In the Shojoji temple garden,
the moon (tsuki) rises.
Everyone come out, come, come, come
many friends."
Then the tanukis beat on their big bellies like a drum (pon pok-a-pon-o).

Ame Fure (Rain Falling)

Music by Nakayama Shinpei, Words by Kitahara Hakushu

Ame, ame, fure, fure, kasan ga.
Janome de omukai ureshii na.
Picchi, picchi, choppu, choppu, ran, ran, ran.

This is a song about a little girl getting out of school and it is raining. She sings:

"Rain, rain, falling, falling, Mother comes
With an umbrella to welcome me and I am happy."
The last line is the sound of raindrops.

Mikazuki Sama (Crescent Moon)

Mikazuki sama, komban wa.
Gitchira, gitchira, koi te.
Yume no o-kuni ni kaeri masho.

This lullaby for young children refers to the crescent
moon as a boat in the sky that can row them to
Dreamland. "Gitchira" is the sound of oars creaking.

"Crescent Moon, Sir, good evening.
Creak, creak, come to us.
Return us to Dreamland."

Sakura (Cherry Blossoms)

Sakura, sakura,
Yayoi no sora wa, miwatasu kagiri.
Kasumi ka kumo ka,
Nioi zo izuru.
Iza ya, iza ya. mi ni yukan.

This is a traditional song about cherry blossoms
blooming in the spring.

"Cherry blossoms, cherry blossoms,
Across the spring sky (sora), as far as I can see.
Like mist (kasumi), like clouds (kumo),
Their fragrance comes.
Let's go, let's go see them."

Moshi, Moshi (Hello, Hello)

Moshi, moshi, ano ne, ano ne, ano ne.
Moshi, moshi, ano ne, ah so, desu ka.

Known as the "Telephone Song," this imitates what
one might overhear when someone speaks on the
phone. It is sung to the tune of "London Bridge is
Falling Down." The translation is:

"Hello, hello, uh huh, uh huh, uh huh.
Hello, hello, uh huh, is that so? I see."

Appendix II

Photographs of Japan
1950's

Courtesy of Allen N. Winter

mother carrying baby,
rice stalks hung to dry along the fence

Boy's Day decorations

picking tea leaves

rice paddies and crop terraces

train ride

washing clothes

vegetable market

hardware store

sign outside Johnson Air Base,
tea bushes and base housing beyond

"Ohka Bomb" kamikaze aircraft
at the entrance to Johnson Air Base

Glossary and Index of Japanese Terms

amezaiku	art of candy-sculpting (20)
arigato	"thank you" (92)
Bon-odori	folk dances of the Obon festival (37)
Buddhism	religion following the thinking of Buddha who believed in living a pure and moral life (36)
geisha	women who were specially trained in how to entertain with singing, dancing and conversation (24, 29)
geta	Japanese-style wooden shoes (7, 82)
haiku	Japanese-style poetry having three lines with 5, 7, and 5 syllables (45)
Hanami	"Flower-Viewing," or Cherry Blossom Festival (26)
haori	short quilted coat (34)
Hina Matsuri	Doll's Day (Girl's Day) Festival (22)
hiragana	in Japanese writing, the set of symbols that stand for basic sounds (46)

ikebana	Japanese style of flower arrangements characterized by simplicity and symbolism (91)
kamishibai	story-theater using large picture-slides shown through an opening in a wooden frame (20)
kamikaze	attacks where a Japanese pilot sacrificed his life using his aircraft or submarine to ram the enemy (68)
kanji	Chinese characters standing for whole words or ideas (46)
karakami	thick paper sliding screens, often painted with beautiful designs (4)
karuta	traditional Japanese New Year's card game (35)
katakana	symbols that stand for special sounds needed for words foreign to the Japanese language (46)
kirigami	Japanese-style art of folding and cutting paper (27)
konnichi wa	"hello" or "good day" (43, 92)
kotatsu	"foot-warmer" made by heating a pit in the floor and covering it with a quilt (10)
miso	soybean paste, used in making soup or other foods (10, 11)
mochi	rice patty made from pounding a special sticky cooked rice into a paste (23, 26, 34)

obi	kimono sash tied or fastened around the waist (25, 37, 51)
Obon	festival to honor the dead (36, 37, 51)
ohayo gozaimasu	"good morning" (polite form) (43)
omikoshi	shrine on a wooden platform that can be lifted and carried through the streets (35)
origami	Japanese art of folding paper (24, 27)
sakura	cherry blossom (26)
sekihan	cooked sticky rice mixed with red beans (23)
sen	similar to an American penny (19, 20, 28)
sensei	teacher (43)
Setsubun	Shinto tradition of chasing away evil spirits (35)
Shinto	native Japanese belief of sacred spirits (gods), good and bad (33, 35, 38)
Shogatsu	New Year Festival (33)
shrine	special place for worshipping a Shinto god said to live in the shrine (17, 21, 23, 24, 33-35, 38, 44, 58)
shushin	system of moral instruction (13, 45, 49)
taiko	very large drums used in festivals (37)

About the Authors –

Yaeko Sugama was born in Japan in 1925. She grew up in the small town of Tokorozawa, near Tokyo, and there experienced the Depression years and World War II. Some years after the war, she met an American serviceman and eventually married him. Her husband then brought her to the United States in 1958 where they settled in Joliet, Illinois, and raised two daughters, Linda and Kathleen. After a divorce and brief second marriage, Ms. Sugama Weldon moved to Madison, Alabama, for a number of years. She currently resides in St. Louis, Missouri. This is her story.

Linda Emiko Austin was born in Chicago in 1959. She was raised on the outskirts of Joliet, Illinois, and schooled in nearby Plainfield. She has many fond memories of visiting Chicago's "Japantown" along North Clark Street as a child, especially the old Star Market grocery and J. Toguri Mercantile, where the scent of incense and the feel of an old-time era of Japan gave her a fascinating window into her Japanese heritage. Linda currently lives with her husband and two daughters in St. Louis, Missouri, with her mother nearby.

Printed in the United States
87258LV00001B/352-486/A

9 780977 232314